THE LOVE OF GOD

A Devotional Book of LOVE, Faith and Miracles, and the
COMING of the Lord

Alma Benefield

Written in LOVE and Inspired by GOD with LOVE

authorHOUSE®

AuthorHouse™
1663 Liberty Drive
Bloomington, IN 47403
www.authorhouse.com
Phone: 1-800-839-8640

First published by AuthorHouse 8/3/2009

ISBN: 978-1-4490-0952-6 (e)
ISBN: 978-1-4389-9880-0 (sc)

Printed in the United States of America
Bloomington, Indiana

This book is printed on acid-free paper.

THEY AIN'T NO GRAVE

Go down yonder Gabriel
Put your foot on the land and sea
Don't you blow that trumpet
Until you hear from me.

Ain't no grave gonna lay this body down
Ain't no grave gonna lay this body down

Well look up yonder in the sky
What is that I see?
I see the King of Kings
He's coming after me

Ain't no grave gonna lay this body down
Ain't no grave gonna lay this body down

Well look up yonder in the sky
What is that I see?
I see a band of angels
Coming after me

Ain't no grave gonna lay this body down
Ain't no grave gonna lay this body down

Take this old body
To the grave yard
Lay this old body down
When Gabriel blows that trumpet
We'll come up out of the ground

Ain't no grave gonna lay this body down
Ain't no grave gonna lay this body down

My husband, Delbert Benefield, who God has chosen to be my soul mate and lifetime partner in the Lord, who saw the vision of the book being published before it was ever completed, wrote this song. He is anointed by God to sing this song. We are not complete without the other.

TABLE OF CONTENTS

ACKNOWLEDGEMENTS

I'd like to say thank you to all those that helped me put together this book and encouraged me. A warm thanks to Kathy Mixson who edited the book for me and had faith in me. Kathy, you are appreciated for the things you do.

For my husband, Delbert, I would like to say a special thank you. He is anointed by God to do a work for God also. He is always on my mind. I know that we are soon going on the greatest journey of our lives. We are pressing toward our vision that was show to both of us at the same time. There will be a Miracle Revival Ministry that will be anointed by God. I'm talking faith for our future. I'm speaking of things as they are not. For faith is the evidence of things not yet seen. I'm talking about faith that has not been fulfilled as of yet. We've been waiting on God for the right time to show us the way. For God's timing is not our timing and our ways are not His ways. For if God is not in it, I know that we will fail. But if God be for us who can be against us?

The word of God says those that wait upon the Lord SHALL renew their strength. They shall mount up with wings as eagles; they shall run and not be weary; and they shall walk and not faint. (Isaiah 41: 31)

Now faith is the substance of things hoped for, the evidence of things not seen. (Hebrews 11:1)

I must have faith to trust God for my ministry and for my book, and believe that it shall be done. For I'm trusting God for great things

May God bless you always.

INTRODUCTION

The Love of God will help teach you and prepare you for the coming of the Lord. It will build your faith and let you know that there is a real God that CAN and WILL do the impossible, if you will only trust God. I am living proof that God is Lord of my life and that God is still performing miracles today. God has put his seal of approval upon this book.

My name is Alma Benefield I was 29 years old when I first wrote this book. I am a Christian that loves God with all my heart, mind and soul. I hope something in this book will help someone draw close to God. Because that is my main desire – to see souls delivered from sin. I don't want anyone to think that I am a big writer, because I am not. This is the first time I have ever tried to write anything before. I am just a normal everyday person that has everyday problems, just like you. All I can say is that I've been through a lot in my life and I know that what God can do for me, he can do for you. I couldn't write this book without God's help and direction in my life.

The book has took twenty two years to get to the point where it is now. A lot of prayer and trusting God, waiting on the Lord to show me the right time for this book to go forth. It sat on a desk for twenty two years, savoring over time until the right time for God to move. I thought it was completed at times, but God said it was not finished yet. Now I understand why I had to wait as long as I did to finish this book. For God was not finished yet. God said I had some things to complete first before the book could be finished.

This book is for the Love of God and people everywhere that need to know God's love in their lives. I love you and God loves you.

Love is the greatest of all gifts.

WHAT GOD HAS DONE FOR US ON THE CROSS

The love of God is strong; if we could only let His love show through us it could touch many lives.

For God so loved the world that he gave his only begotten son, that whosoever believeth in him should not perish but have everlasting life. (John 3:16)

For God's love is one of the greatest commandments of all mankind. Because He says to love thy neighbor as thyself and love thy neighbor, as you would have them love you, in Christ Jesus.

For without God's love for us He could not have gave His only begotten son to die on that old rugged cross at Calvary. For God had His son to die on that cross so that we could have eternal life and could have forgiveness of sin.

But God, who is rich in mercy, for His great love wherewith He loved us. (Ephesians 2:4) Grace be to you and peace from God the Father and from our Lord Jesus Christ, who gave himself for our sins, that he might deliver us from this present evil world, according to the will of God and our Father. (Galatians 1:3-4) In whom we have redemption through his blood, the forgiveness of sins according to the riches of his grace. (Ephesians 1:7)

I would like to take a few minutes to tell you what the Bible says about Jesus death at Calvary. First they stripped him of his clothes and put him on a scarlet robe. Then they beat him and placed a crown of thorns upon his head, and they spit on him. He carried his cross up to Calvary where they nailed his hands and feet to a cross for you and me. Then, as he was hanging there, they offered him vinegar mixed with gall for him to drink of it. There they yelled to him, "If you be the Son of God sent to save the world then save yourself from this horrible death. Then Jesus cried unto the Lord with a loud voice, *"Forgive them, for they know not what they do."* Then he cried unto the Lord, *"Why hast thou forsaken me?"* Then Jesus cried with another loud voice and gave up the ghost.

But even though they beat him until blood was dripping down his side, God knew that would be the way it would have to be according to the prophecy. But every stripe upon his back was for our healings. That we could be healed by the blood of Jesus Christ. That by his stripes we are healed by the blood of Jesus Christ.

God paid an awful price for us when he suffered and died for us on Calvary. Shouldn't we love Him enough to love one another without judging that person? For judge not lest you be judged at the judgment. But love thy neighbor as thy self. That means that no matter what that person does you are to forgive that person, for that is the way the Lord would have it to be. Love that person just the same, for we are all God's children and he loves us all just the same. Love is forgiving others for what they do. For love is the greatest thing that we can have in our life.

Put on therefore, as the elect of God, holy and beloved, bowels of mercies, kindness, humbleness of mind, meekness, longsuffering; Forbearing one another and forgiving one another, if any man have a quarrel against any: even as Christ forgave you, so also do ye. And above all these things put on charity, which is love, which is the bond of perfectness. (Colossians 3: 12 – 14)

That Christ may dwell in your hearts by faith; that ye, being rooted and grounded in love. (Ephesians 3:17) And to know the love of Christ which passeth knowledge, that ye might be filled with all the fullness of God. (Ephesians 3:19) In whom we have redemption through his blood, the forgiveness of sins, according to the riches of his grace. (Ephesians 1:7) For by grace are ye saved through faith and that not of yourself, it is the gift of God. (Ephesians 2:8) And be ye kind one to another, tenderhearted, forgiving one another, even as God for Christ sake hath forgiven you. (Ephesians 4:32)

Walk in love, as Christ also hath loved us and hath given himself for us an offering and a sacrifice to God for a sweet-smelling savour. (Ephesians 5:2) Peace be to the brethren and love with faith, from God the Father and the Lord Jesus Christ. Grace be with all them that love our Lord Jesus Christ in sincerity. (Ephesians 6:23 – 24) And this is his commandment, That we should believe on the name of his Son Jesus Christ and love one another, as he gave us commandment. (I John 3:23)

Beloved let us love one another: for love is of God; and every one that loveth is born of God and knoweth God. He that loveth not knoweth not God; for God is love. In this was manifested the love of God toward us, because that God sent his only begotten Son into the world that we might live through him. Herein is love, not that we love God but that he loved us and sent his Son to be the propitiation for our sins. Beloved if God so loved us, we ought also to love one another. If we love one another, God dwelleth in us, and his love is perfected in us. (I John 4: 7-12)

We love him, because he first loved us. (I John 4:19)

We are supposed to love our wives and our husbands.

Wives submit yourselves unto your own husband, as it is fit in the Lord. Husbands love your wives and be not bitter against them. (Colossians 3: 18 – 19)

But I say unto you, Love your enemies, bless them that curse you, do good to them that hate you, and pray for them which despitefully use you, and persecute you; That ye may be the children of your Father which is in Heaven: for he maketh his sun to rise on the evil and on the good, and sendeth rain on the just and on the unjust. For if you love them which love you, what reward have you? do not even the publicans the same? (Matthew 5: 44 – 46)

For if ye forgive men their trespasses, your heavenly Father will also forgive you: But if ye forgive not men their trespasses, neither will your Father forgive your trespasses. (Matthew 6: 14 – 15)

You may ask how many times should we forgive a person for what they do?

In Matthew 18: 22,

Jesus saith unto him, I say not unto thee, Until seven times: but Until seventy times seven we are to forgive that person of what they do.

For you have to forgive that person in order to make it into the kingdom of God. You cannot love the world and serve God. For you can't serve God and man. Don't live by man, but live for God only. For God is a God that wants you to serve Him and Him only. Serve God with all your heart, mind and soul. For God is a God that never changes. He is always the same today, yesterday, and forever. God never changes, people change, and let things come ahead of God. Put Him first and you will find that He is always there with outstretched arms. Anything you ask in his name it SHALL be added unto you. But ahead of everything seek ye first the kingdom of God, and anything in His name you ask, it SHALL be given unto you.

HOW TO MAKE IT THROUGH YOUR VALLEYS

Loving God is loving someone that we cannot see. But at the same time, we can feel His presence when we're going through things we can't understand. Sometimes God puts us in a position where we have to call upon His name for help, for we can't do it alone. Sometimes this is called being in a valley. All you have to say is, "Lord, have mercy on me and help me make it through this valley," and He will be there for you. But when you're in the valley, the Lord has a chance to talk to you. From time to time, God puts us in the valley where He can really talk to us and show us things that we may not have seen before we were in the valley.

But remember these words when you find yourself in the valley, that He made us a promise. He said that you should not let your heart become troubled with the things of this world. But He promised us He would be with us even until the end of the world. God sometimes puts us in the valley to chastise us and see if we will draw nigh unto Him. For God is our strength when we come against things we can't solve on our own. Just carry it to God first and see if He won't give you strength and show you the way out of the situation. For without God's love, where would we be today? For God is our hope for tomorrow.

Here is a promise from God that we should pass on to others and lift up others with these words:

For I have gone to prepare a place for you that where I am there you may be also. For I will come back for those that are prayed up and doing the will of my Father which is in heaven.

To comfort one another with these words at all times that they may not forget that He will come back to receive us unto His bosom. But most of all, pray without ceasing, for now is the time to do a work for God, for time is drawing nigh. For not even the angels in heaven know of His coming. But it is much closer than you think.

For God is a jealous God that only inhabits your praise and your love. But no man can serve two masters, for either he will hate the one and despise the other. Ye cannot serve God and mammon, which is man. This means either you love God or you love Satan, but it is your choice. It is impossible to serve God and man at the same time. Either you serve God or you let Satan cheat you out of your blessings that God has in store for you.

For Satan can confuse you in many ways and make you think God is not the answer to your problems. Satan will lie and deceive you to get your mind off of God. Satan will put thoughts in your mind that you would not otherwise have on your mind to get your eyes off God. Satan just will not let you think that God is good, but will try to keep you from ever being close to God. He will put thoughts in your mind that you would not otherwise have on your mind. Some of these thoughts may be about using drugs or alcohol, and sometimes make you believe that you have some kind of disease that is incurable. This is just to get our minds off of God and get our minds on our circumstances.

Sometimes Satan tricks us into doing things that we do not want to do. Such things as committing suicide, which is not of God but of Satan. But suicide will never be the answer to the problem. For Jesus is the answer to all our needs today. All we have to do is ask God to come into our hearts and ask God's forgiveness and let Him come into our hearts to dwell forever. Then we have the opportunity to get Satan out of our lives and live a holy and consecrated life unto the Lord. For God is our deliverer of all things that may get in the way of keeping us holy unto the Lord. Praise God at all times and give Him the praise for everything. And He will inhabit your praise unto Him. But you do not have to be bound with drugs, alcohol, or anything that you may think may be unholy to God. For my God CAN do all things, for there is nothing impossible with God to those that believe in miracles.

My God has once been put to death by the world but Praise God, my God is not dead no more. For God lives today and forever. For my God's not dead, but He is alive today. He is as real to me as He was when He went about the wayside preaching the gospel.

Believe that I died and arose on that third day and believe ye that I am sitting on the right hand of the Father which is in heaven. I will come and get those that are prayed up and ready to go. For be ye ready and prayed up and doing the will of my Father which is in heaven. For be ye ready should he come today. For there may come a day that it may be too late to call on my name.

HOW TO BELIEVE AND EXPECT A MIRACLE

God's love can be so special to those that will let it. For God's love should always come first in our lives. God's love can let us be closer to Him. Even closer than a mother, a father, a brother or a sister. For God can be a comfort when you're in trouble. So remember when you're in trouble and you can't solve it on your own that God is the answer to every need that you may have in your life. Even if you're bound with things beyond your control. Just turn these things over to God no matter what the problem.

My God can still do miracles today as He did in the Bible long ago. For all He really wants you to do is admit that you have a problem so He can help you with the problem that you have. Then we must pray and ask God to show us the way out of the problem so that we can receive our deliverance miracle from God. But most of all we should ask God's forgiveness and ask Him to come into our heart. Then we must strive to do what God wants us to do. But nothing is impossible to those that believe in miracles. If you believe in miracles then you can believe that God wants you to have everything you ask him for in the name of Jesus.

But first seek ye the kingdom of God and all these other things will be added unto you. But there is deliverance for all those that want deliverance, even if it is from drugs, alcohol or any other thing that does not please God. Then we should seek God's direction in our lives. For my God can deliver you from anything if you will trust Him for a miracle of deliverance.

My friend, you have got to want deliverance before God can do anything for you. Then don't let anyone stand in the way to stop you from getting your miracle. Believe with all your heart, mind and soul that the answer is on the way. Even though things all around you are going wrong. But be patient for the answer and the answer will come when you least expect it to. Just keep praying for that miracle in the name of Jesus. Then stand back and watch the salvation of the Lord work in your life. When you think that you are about to give up, the answer will come. Never give up for your miracle for it will come.

Just call on me and I will hear your cry when in time of need. Look to me for all things and it will be added unto you.

All you have to do is believe and all things are possible to those that put their trust in me. God performed a miracle when he led the people out of the land of Egypt. For they were bound as slaves and God sent Moses to deliver then out of bondage. Many other times God performed miracles for people. God gave David strength to kill a giant twice his size. God delivered the three Hebrew children form the fiery furnace, so that not even a hair on their head was singed. They didn't even smell of smoke because they trusted God and God came to their rescue and walked with them through that fiery furnace.

God delivered Daniel out of the lion's den. God locked the lion's mouth so that the lion could not harm Daniel, and Daniel laid down and slept on the lion's belly that night. God again delivered Joshua from a mighty army and caused the walls of Jericho to come tumbling down so that he would not have to fight. God told Joshua to march around Jericho six days and not say a word, but on the seventh day to "*blow the trumpet and start praising me and I will fight your battle for you.*"

Again God delivered Jonah from the belly of the whale. For God chastised Jonah to see if he would do what he was told to do.

God performed many miracles through Moses. First he caused Moses to turn his staff into a snake because Pharaoh would not let the people go. Then he caused the water to turn to blood with the touch from his staff to the water. Moses called on God to feed the people after Pharaoh had let the people out of bondage. God sent manna down from heaven and meat for them to eat. Again Moses called on the Lord to help him cross the Red Sea and the water began to divide so that they could cross over to the other side. God protected Moses and the people many times.

These are just a few miracles God did in the Old Testament.

In the New Testament Jesus told Peter to "cast a hook and take up the fish that first cometh up and when thou hast opened his mouth thou shalt find a piece of money, that take and give unto them for me and thee."

Then Jesus began to pray for those that was possessed with unclean spirits and they were delivered.

Then Jesus began to pray for those that was deaf and dumb and they were delivered. He prayed for those that was blind and could not see and they were healed.

God commanded those to come from the grave that was dead and they did come alive.

God performed a miracle when he fed a multitude of people with five loaves of bread and two little fishes and fed five thousand people and had twelve baskets left over.

Again God fed the people with seven loaves of bread and five little fishes. This time He fed four thousand people and had seven baskets left over.

Jesus performed another miracle when He healed a man that had palsy and could not walk.

The purpose of all these miracles from the Bible is to convince you to start believing in miracles. For there is nothing too big or small that God can't do. If God can deliver a man possessed with an unclean spirit, why can't you believe that God can deliver you from drugs and alcohol? You CAN be delivered, just call upon the Lord and ask him for deliverance. Ask God for deliverance and see what God will do for you.

I want you to understand that no matter what the problem, God can still deliver you out. For God can be your way out of terrible situations. Just trust Him for whatever you need and have the faith of the grain of a mustard seed and you CAN be delivered. The key is just in believing that all things are possible with God to those that believe in Him. So remember when you come to a situation you cannot handle on your own, place it on the alter and leave it there. Put it in the hands of God and let God bring you out. But trust God and carry everything before Him in prayer and you will find that you will get an answer from God when you may not be able to find an answer on your own.

Have faith in God. Trust him for everything and you will find that all things will be added unto you. Trust, believe in God and see what God can do for you. For there is nothing too big or too small for God. Trust God, believe with faith. For you must have faith to receive a miracle. You must have courage to ask God for help. For all things are possible to those that believe in miracles.

Even now I have to believe in a miracle like I never have before, because it will take faith to believe in a miracle for my Daughter. I have recently found out that she has a disease called Turner's Syndrome. That has caused her to have problems growing to the extent that she may not never mature to be a young woman and may not ever be able to have a child of her own. This syndrome causes other complications such as mental retardation, thyroid problems, heart problems and even diabetes.

But I am going to wait for God to perform the miracle at his own appointed time. For that is the only thing I can do -- pray and keep believing for her miracle. I do not know the time nor the hour, but I do believe that she will be healed. For I believe in miracles and I do not believe in unbelief. For God has brought me through many things and healed me of a nerve condition and I know what God can do. I wish I could tell you about my miracle for her, but until it happens, I can't.

MIRACLES IN MY LIFE

A brother in my church had been in a very bad car wreck. The wreck was so bad it completely destroyed his car and he was trapped inside the car. The paramedics had to pry the car door to get him out of the car. When they got this man out of the car, they found that half of his face had been torn off and thought that he was going to bleed to death. They even thought he would not make it to the hospital. Immediately people in the church began to pray for him. But during the time he was in the hospital his wife would not let anyone pray for him that did not have the faith to believe for a miracle. At the hospital, they put him in surgery and repaired his face with plastic surgery. Today this man is still alive and serving God, testifying to others about how God delivered him from that wreck. To me he is truly a miracle.

I have experienced many miracles in my life. At the age of fifteen I became very ill with a very high fever that would not come down. I was so sick I could not even walk because I was so weak. I couldn't eat because I had no appetite. I thank God for my boyfriend, who now is my husband, that he prayed all night for God to heal me. Thank God, He did heal me. I have never been that sick with a fever since that time.

Again, after having my babies I had trouble with female infections. It became so bad that I felt my insides were coming out. I went to doctors every two months with this problem, but nothing seemed to help. The infection would just keep coming back. I had doctors tell me several times that I needed an operation. I went three years with this problem with hardly any relief for the pain. But one night in church, the preacher called me out and said that God was going to heal my organs. God healed me that night and, Praise God, it has been years since I have had any infection in my organs.

Again, God healed me of a problem with my stomach. I would wake up throwing up and would be sick two and three days a week. I went to see the doctor but he could not find what the problem was. They thought I had a gas pocket in my stomach. I went for months having pains in my stomach and throwing up all the time. But God healed me of that too.

God healed me of a nervous condition where the doctors said I was having a nervous breakdown. Have you ever had a seizure? If you have then you will know what I'm going to be talking about. I had just come home from a trip to Mayport and when I got home I felt very tired. So I went in and laid down on my bed. After I laid down, my body started jerking and I could not stop the jerking. I called my husband and he called the Rescue to take me to the hospital.

When they got there I was still having some jerking. They asked me if I could walk and I said I'd try. But when I went to walk I couldn't because my legs were like jelly. I went to the hospital and they did not really know what was wrong with me. They diagnosed me as having a nervous breakdown. They gave me a sedative to get me to rest. They sent me home and told me to go see a psychologist. But I never did go see a psychologist and I never will. But I am so glad God healed me of this problem.

Sometimes the Devil tries to put this nervous condition back on me. But the Devil is a Liar and the Father of it. For I will continue to rebuke Satan as long as he tries to destroy me. I give God the Glory for healing me. I still suffer a bit of pain in my body. There is not a day hardly that goes by that I'm not in pain somewhere in my body. Satan has tried for years to destroy me just because I serve God with all my heart, mind and soul.

As long as the Devil fights, I'm going to continue to serve God no matter what it takes. I will fight Satan with everything that is within me to make it into heaven because I refuse to go back in this sinful world without God. For knowing God is what comforts me through all the pain and the suffering that I go through. It is worth it all to me just to be able to serve God.

⌒

My brother was in an accident in Daytona. He was hit by a truck while riding a bike. He was taken to Halifax Hospital in Daytona as a John Doe. He had some ID on him, but the hospital did not know how to get in touch with the family. Finally my brother's boss contacted my other brother, James, and told him that his brother was in an accident. That he might have to go and verify his identity. James went to Halifax Hospital to identify my baby brother, Tom. He had suffered from a head injury and a crushed wrist and a fractured collarbone.

When James got to the hospital, he was told that Tom had fluid on his brain and that there might be a blood clot. Tom's head looked like a basketball. He was almost impossible to identify due to the swelling of his brain. Within 24 hours after his accident the hospital called the family to let us know that Tom was going to need emergency surgery on his brain due to the blood clot rupturing the brain and that if they did not do the surgery right away he could die.

I was working for Salvation Army at the time when I got the call. I told my supervisor I needed to go to the hospital. I left my job and picked up my mother and we headed to Daytona. I drove 80 mph all the way hoping I would not get caught speeding on the way there. When we arrived at the hospital they were waiting for someone to sign the paperwork to do his surgery.

Tom was in surgery for a long time. Doctors came out to tell us that they had lost him on the operating table and had to resuscitate him. He was out of danger, however, and the surgery went well. They had to put metal plates in his forehead due to the fact that the front part of the forehead was destroyed. He made it through the surgery and was in an Intensive Care room for a week. They kept asking him what his name was and the date. Can you imaging getting in an accident on your birthday? It was April 5th of 1997. He had cake in the hospital room. But he was lucky to be alive. We was glad we had the opportunity to be with him again.

When it came time for him to go to a Rehabilitation Center, Tom needed a family member to keep a close eye on him due to him being confused and disoriented. He could walk at the time and talk. When he walked he would walk as if he was off balance, but thank God he could walk and talk. He still had to have surgery on his wrist. Guess who was there through it all -- yes, his big sister.

I traveled back and forth to Daytona for weeks trying to work my job and be there for my brother. It began to be too much for me so I left my job to take care of him. When it came time for him to leave Rehab he had to be with someone at all times. He could not be left alone. But the doctors said he could not be around a family with young kids due to him being confused all the time. So I moved him to Macclenny and he stayed with me for a whole year during his recovery.

He had to have three surgeries on his wrist trying to get his wrist back to what it should be. But even with all their efforts to repair the wrist it was still not normal. They ended up having to put three metal plates in his arm. I never left his side through every surgery, through his physical therapy, through even talking to his lawyers and his doctors.

I've never had any experiences with lawyers before until this accident happened. I did learn a lot about similar cases. For example, if you do not have a head witness to get bought out from the other party, that you do not have a case.

There was many times my brother would have seizures and not know who he was or where he was. He would have no idea what to do. God led me to introduce myself to him as his sister Alma and to tell him who he was. Then from there I introduced my husband and the children, each by their names.

Every seizure he had was different. I had to take notes on every seizure he had to tell his doctors, so they would know how to treat him.

During this time, most of my trips to Daytona were spent in doctors' offices and hospitals trying to find out all I could about my brother's situation. The doctors told me he could become violent at times. There were times that I was afraid of him, because he would walk past me and say that he would like to hit me.

God protected me the whole time I took care of my brother. My brother never did become violent. But I had to watch him all the time and make sure he did not hurt himself during a seizure episode.

I learned a lot about head injuries and trauma to the brain and wrist repair: That if a wrist is crushed beyond repair that they have to place metal plates and pins in the bones hoping the bone will grow back together.

I want you to know I am not bragging on me, but I am bragging on God. God helped me deal with every problem and every situation that came up. Every day I had to pray for strength to take care of my brother. But I've said all this to let you know that if God tells you to do something for Him, He will equip you to do what He told you to do.

God told me to quit my job and take care of my brother. Not to worry about my finances – that He would take care of my needs. That he wanted me to get along with him and pray and read the Word. For He had called me to take care of those who cannot take care of themselves. Would you believe that God supplied food, gas, and anything else I needed? I never done without food, gas or money. God blessed me in so many ways. When you humble yourself before God and are obedient to Him, He will take care of you.

I nursed my brother back to health, and now he has been taking care of his own needs. He has worked several different jobs. He worked in telemarketing, he has been a manager at Hardee's, and now he's working at a truck stop.

But God has a call upon my brother's life, even though he does not know it yet. Or then again, he may know, but he is running from God. God is so good to those that love the Lord.

⟶

January of 1975, before my husband and me was married, my husband was electrocuted by 17,000 watts of electricity. He and his brother were putting up an antenna on top of a trailer. It was raining at the time and somehow the electric line arched toward the antenna. My husband and his brother hit the ground. My husband had shoes on and his brother didn't, so my husband was grounded. His brother somehow was slung up against the trailer.

My husband was on the ground close to death when he said he heard the most beautiful singing he had ever heard. Something said, "look toward the light" and God began to bring him to. See, he had a near death experience. But God was not through with him yet.

The only damage my husband received was that the electricity went out through his little toe and he had small spots in his hands. His brother suffered more damage because he was not grounded. He suffered nerve damage in his right hand. He had to have several operations to repair the damage. They are both miracles of God. God spared their lives from 17,000 watts of electricity. They are both walking miracles.

DELIVERANCE FROM DRUGS, ALCOHOL
AND ABORTION

My friend, you do not have to be bound by a drug. Sometimes people try drugs thinking that they can find peace. But my friend, drugs will destroy your mind and make you do things such as committing suicide. My friend, you can never find a way out of your problems by using drugs. By taking drugs to solve your problems you will only allow more problems. But drugs will destroy you and destroy your family. When you're using drugs you lose all perspective of the things around you. You just don't care anymore. You will lie and do anything you can to get these drugs, not realizing or even thinking about what you do to your family until it's too late. After you're hooked on the drugs it is hard to stop on your own.

My friend, there is hope for you. Being spaced out on drugs is not cool. Seeing things that are not there is not what God wants for us. God wants us to have a clear, clean mind and be holy as He is holy.

For be ye holy as I am holy. For I am the Lord of Lords and King of all Kings. I am the Alpha, the Omega and the Bright and Morning Star. Believe that I CAN heal you of drugs. For there is nothing too big that I can't do.

My friend, please don't destroy yourself by using drugs. For drugs kill everybody and everything around you. I write about this topic because I want you to know that I am someone who cares about you. Remember, there is a God willing to help you anytime you ask Him to.

My friend, I know what alcohol can do to a family. I have lived around drinking most all of my life. But after I married my husband, I decided that I didn't want to be around it any more. Things was so bad in my life as a child I prayed every night that God would get me out of the mess my family had created for me. So at seventeen I married to get out of the mess I was in. Don't get me wrong -- I didn't just marry my husband because I wanted a way out. I married him because I loved him very much. But I was at the end of my rope. I had took all I could take.

I always wanted a Christian family. So I prayed that God would send me a Christian husband, and He did.

I am so glad and thankful for a husband that doesn't drink, because I honestly believe that I could not stand to live with another alcoholic. Till today I cannot get close to my father because when he drinks he begins to think about the past. I want more than anything for him to stop drinking. His problem with drinking has caused a problem with our relationship. His problem has caused me a lot of insecurity in my life. He has always blamed things on me when he was drinking and that has hurt me very much. Sometimes I would find myself hating him because of what he had done to my family. Because his drinking destroyed my mother and father's marriage of seventeen years. That, I feel, could have been avoided if he had just quit drinking and seeing other women.

It took me a long time to get over the hurt of what my father's drinking had done to us. It took a long time to forgive him and just to tell him that I loved him. But if it hadn't been for the Love of God in my life, I might have still went on hating him.

I just wish he would have been there for me more than he was. I miss the things that we could have done together if he had not been gone so much. I want more than anything for us to be able to have a close relationship, but I know that will never happen because he can't let loose of the past. Many times I could not talk to him and really tell him how I felt because I was afraid to say anything to him. How can you really talk to anyone when they're under the influence of alcohol? To prevent me from being hurt I always agreed with him, no matter if it was true or not. Many times my father would tell me he didn't love me. That was very hard for me to take sometimes. I finally began thinking that he really didn't love me.

So you see that I know how alcohol destroys a family. For I sat back and watched it destroy my family everyday. But I can't talk to my father about this problem. When I tried to defend myself he thought I was trying to be smart with him. So a month or two went by and I thought I would try to see him again. There I was in front of a bunch of people and he cursed and called me all kinds of ugly words. But at the time, he was drinking when he said these things. So I've decided just to stay away from him until he can apologize to me. I still love him very much, but I cannot continue to be hurt by him any more.

So, my friend, please do not destroy your family and loved ones by throwing your life away on alcohol. I've been there and I know what it will do to a family. It not only destroys the family but destroys the love that family has toward one another. So please ask God to help you whip the problem of alcohol before it destroys you and your family. Your family deserves to have the best days of your life. They can't have the best days of your life if you're drunk all the time. God wants us to be sober-minded and not drunk on wine.

Remember this – God loves you! No matter what you've done. Just ask God to help you and He will. For He has never turned his back on anyone that asked Him to do something for them.

Just knock and the door will be opened unto you, ask and you SHALL receive anything in my name. For, yea I am at the door waiting for you to ask for my help.

God can do nothing until you make up your mind to make things better in your life. But my friend, God is a deliverer of all things no matter what it is. Just trust God and see if he will not open the windows of heaven and pour you out a blessing you cannot receive.

That if thou shalt confess with thy mouth the Lord Jesus, and shalt believe in thine heart that God hath raised him from the dead, thou shalt be saved. (Romans 10:9) For whosoever shall call upon the name of the Lord SHALL be saved. (Romans 10:13) I beseech you therefore, brethren, by the mercies of God, that ye present your bodies a living sacrifice, holy, acceptable unto God, which is your reasonable service. (Romans 12:1)

For I say, through the grace given unto me, to every man that is among you, not to think of himself more highly than he ought to think; but to think soberly, according as God hath dealt to every man the measure of faith. (Romans 12:3) For it is written, As I live, saith the Lord, every knee SHALL bow to me, and every tongue confess to God. (Romans 14:11)

Abortions are like killing someone, even if you think that baby doesn't deserve to live. Everyone deserves to have a chance to live, I don't care what anyone says. A baby alive inside you is the most beautiful thing I know. Do you know that even a baby at three months in the womb of a mother already has its arms legs and head, and has already developed its body? That baby is very much alive growing inside of you. Sure you may not be able to feel that baby until you're four months pregnant, but that baby is living and surviving off of you. That baby is a part of you.

Do you know that millions of babies die because women have abortions? Think before you decide to have an abortion, that when you have an abortion you are killing your unborn baby. And the loss of that child you will never forget -- the pain that you went through for the loss of your baby. Before you have an abortion, stop and think about that baby growing inside you. It deserves to live too.

Please if you are thinking to abort a child, there are other options. You can give the child up for adoption. There are many families and women that cannot have a baby that would be glad to adopt your baby. Then there is another option – you can decide to keep you baby and love that baby. For after all, it is part of you.

My God, please don't kill my little babies. But if you have an abortion, God will forgive you and give you peace of mind. God can wipe away all the guilt and shame and make you feel like a person again. A lot of people do not know that they use aborted babies in shampoo and make-up products every day. The reason I know this is because I studied about what they do with unborn babies that were aborted. I studied all this at the college I went to. So all these facts are true. God wants these babies to live.

Please don't kill my little babies for they are one of my little ones. God looks down on His little ones as special. Please, give these babies a chance to live for they are precious to me as you are precious to me. Remember God is willing to forgive you of anything no matter what you've done. For my God is a just God and is not one to judge you of what you do. Remember, I care about these babies and I love you just the way you are.

Jesus is the answer to all your problems that you may have in your life today and in the future. Trust and be honest with yourself and carry them to God instead of others, for He is the only one that can solve your problems. For just ask and you SHALL receive, knock and the door SHALL be opened unto you. These words have always helped me during my Christian life. I've found He has never failed me yet. For He can do anything, just give him a chance to give you a chance to receive what he has for you.

For God has everything. God can solve any problem - just ask Him to help you with the problem. I'm sure He'll make a way of escape for you. He made a way for me when I'd been down in the valley. I had a lot on my mind and thought I didn't have any hope. But you wouldn't believe what He done for me. He took all the pain away that I had. He told me what to do about the problem, so I done what He said and He filled my heart with love again and gave me a chance to go on.

I'm God all over the mountains, I'm God all over the hills, and God all over creation. I'm God when you're in the valley. Tell me your troubles and I SHALL lift you back on that mountain. Just remember, I'll never forsake you if you put your faith in me. For I am everywhere. I know your deepest thoughts and the love that you have for me. I always know what you desire. Just ask of me for your needs and it SHALL be given unto you. For that is a promise that I have written in my scriptures, to let my children know that if you knock on my door and ask, you SHALL receive. Put your faith in me and I will give you everlasting life forever. Thus saith the Lord Thy God!

A BETTER WAY BESIDES SUICIDE

Even now as I write this story of the love of God, I have been in the valley. I have just about hit rock bottom with everything going wrong. I feel I am going through the deepest valley I have ever been in, but I am not giving up hope yet. For I believe with all my heart that my miracle is on the way. Without God comforting me I could not make it through this valley. For God has showed me a promise of tomorrow and at this time, those promises are all I have to hold on to.

I have tried solving my problems before by trying to commit suicide. But I know now that is not the answer to my problems. The answer to my problem is the love of God in my life. If you feel you can't make it on your own and you feel that suicide is the answer my friend, stop and think first. My friend, turn it over to God first, for if you commit suicide without asking God to forgive you then my friend you will die in hell forever! For suicide is not of God, but of Satan. For it is his job to seek and destroy who he can.

But Satan does not like it when you go to God first. Then believe by faith it will get better. My friend it will get better if you turn it over to God first. For God's love can do so much for a person that does not know where to turn. Even my faith has growed during this trial that I am going through, but I keep believing with all my heart and trusting God that I will receive my miracle.

My promise from God came when I least expected it to come. But my miracle from God came just in time. We was almost two months behind on our trailer payments and thought we was going to have to move. I knew I didn't have the money to move with, but we had looked and couldn't find anything.

The week before my answer I had given a love offering of $50.00 to the church and put on the envelope "expecting a miracle from God." I gave that money by faith even though that was all I had. By the end of that week, I received a check for my daughter for $1,270.54. We never expected it to be that much but it was. We had enough to pay our payments and a lot of other things we didn't have the money to pay before. But my prayer was answered because I had faith enough to believe. Faith is the key to receiving all miracles.

HOW TO HAVE A RELATIONSHIP WITH GOD

The love of God can be strong or weak, it all depends on you. If you want a strong relationship with the Lord, you have to call on the Lord. If you pray for a closer relationship with the Lord, then you will have a strong relationship with God. But if you don't pray much and seek God, you will have a weak relationship with God. God expects us to call on Him all the time, not part of the time. With God, we can have strong love or weak love, but with God it CAN be strong. But without God, the love of God is weak. I want nothing more than for you to have the love of God strong in your life as it is in mine, because I truly love God with all my heart, mind and soul.

Because this is the only way He wants us to love him - all the time. God is good and His love is good. Just try it and see what God can do for you. But we have got to pray without ceasing and never falter, to have the love of God dwelling in us. Because we need God's love as much as He needs our love. But His love is greater than any other love, even the love of a husband or a loved one. Because He wants us to love Him as He has loved us.

For God is God and He will always be God. For God is a God that never changes. He's the same today, yesterday, and forever. For God is a God that changeth not. For we were the ones that changed, not God.

HOW TO MOVE MOUNTAINS IN YOUR LIFE

Sometimes we have obstacles that get in our lives that may seem like mountains that can't be moved. Anything that gets your mind off of serving God may be a mountain in your life. The mountains are strong, but cast your cares unto the Lord and leave them there. For when we try to do things ourselves we sometimes do and say the wrong things. But God knows everything we do and say at all times. But God can always do a better job. For I say nothing is impossible with God to those that believe. Just believe it, accept, and it's yours in the name of Jesus. For the spirit is strong but the flesh is weak. But all things are possible to those that believe in miracles.

For God so loved the world that he gave his only begotten son, that whosoever believeth in him should not perish but have everlasting life. (John 3:16)

God gave us authority to say, "Get behind me Satan" in the name of Jesus, and He also gave us the authority to move mountains.

For verily I say unto you that whosoever shall say unto this mountain, Be thou removed, and be thou cast into the sea; and shall not doubt in his heart, but shall believe that those things which he saith SHALL come to pass, he SHALL have whatsoever he saith. Therefore, I say unto you, What things soever ye desire, when ye pray, believe that ye receive them, and ye SHALL have them. (Mark 11:23 – 24)

And Jesus said unto them, Because of your unbelief: for verily I say unto you, If ye have faith as a grain of mustard seed, ye shall say unto this mountain, Remove hence to yonder place, and it SHALL remove; and nothing shall be impossible unto you. (Matthew 17:20) Jesus answered and said unto them, Verily I say unto you, If ye have faith, and doubt not, ye shall not only do this which is done to the fig tree, but also if ye shall say unto this mountain, Be thou removed, and be thou cast into the sea; it SHALL be done. And all things, whatsoever ye shall ask in prayer, believing, ye SHALL receive. (Matthew 21:21 – 22)

For God is not the author of confusion but the Comforter when we are in trouble. For God is a wonder working God. For my God CAN do anything.

HOW BEAUTIFUL HEAVEN IS AND WHAT WE CAN LOOK FORWARD TO

We come from a world of sin and cross over into eternal life. For heaven is worth it all, my friend. For heaven is a place we will never have to worry anymore, or be sick. And the tears we shed here, there will be no more crying there.

For God said I have gone to prepare a place for you. If it were not so, I would not have told you so. For in my house are many mansions, for where I am there you may be also.

For heaven to me is beyond compare to anything here below. Just think about streets that are paved with pure gold, gates that are made of pearl, and every stone will have its place there. Even more beautiful than I have ever seen before. Those that has died with sickness will have a brand new body. For you will be known there as you are known now. For all this CAN be yours my friend. Just commit yourself unto Him and all these things will be added unto you in heaven. Let God lead you in the right direction and I promise you will never regret letting him lead you in the path of righteousness.

In the Bible it says in Revelation 21:4 – 6:

God SHALL wipe away all tears from their eyes; and there SHALL be no more death, neither sorrow, nor crying, neither SHALL there be any more pain: for the former things are passed away. I am Alpha and Omega, the beginning and the end. I will give unto him that is athirst of the fountain of the water of life freely. And the building of the wall of it was of jasper: and the city was pure gold, like unto clear glass. And the foundations of the wall of the city were garnished with all manner of precious stones. (Revelations 21:18 – 19)

And the twelve gates were twelve pearls: every several gate was of one pearl: and the street of the city was pure gold, as it were transparent glass. And I saw no temple therein: for the Lord God Almighty and the Lamb are the temple of it.

And the city had no need of the sun, neither of the moon, to shine in it: for the glory of God did lighten it, and the Lamb is the light thereof. (Revelations 21: 21 – 23)

And all these things CAN be yours to those that believe Jesus is the light and the Bright and Morning Star. This place that I took from the scriptures is a place called Heaven.

A TIME TO WORK FOR GOD

Now is the time, my friend, to commit yourself unto God. For if we should stand and wait too long it may be too late to call upon the name of the Lord. My friend, God has a special plan for all those that commit themselves unto him. But if you don't call upon the Lord to show you these things, then you will never know what you are to do for God. For the love of God is greater than any other love. A time with God is like a thousand years. Once time is gone we cannot turn back the hands of time to start all over. So if you feel God is calling you, don't put it off for tomorrow, because tomorrow may be too late. Once you commit yourself to God then you will see things start to happen. But don't think there will not be trials, because there will be. Being a Christian and serving God is not always smelling the roses. But the best time in my life has been since I became a Christian, and since I started serving God.

The main reason I wrote this book is because I love you and I want you to understand the love of God. Another reason is because God said to write it, so that is what I'm doing. Otherwise, I have committed myself to writing this book. Committing yourself is being willing to go all the way with God. That no matter what he says to do, be willing to go and do for the Lord. When you become saved you have committed yourself to give up all things that are in the world and to follow him. And to pay the price no matter what it may be. If it's singing for God or preaching the gospel to the people, just be willing to do for God and he will be your strength in time of trouble.

For there may be a time it may be too late to do that which is of the Father:

Know ye that I am the master, King of Kings and Lord of Lords. For I am the Alpha the Omega and the Beginning and the End. That where I am there you may be also. For believe that I am with the Father which is in heaven. For low, I stand and knock at the door, waiting for you to ask for forgivings of your sins. So that I can free you from the world. For I would rather have you free from sin.

For my God is the deliverer of all things. Try God and see what He has in store for you.

For I am not the author of confusion, but the deliverer to those that believe that I died on the cross and arose from the grave the third day.

Work while it is day. For time is running out. Work for God while it is still day. Because there may be a day that it may be too late to pray for salvation of the Lord.

For low, I come as a thief in the night.

So pray without ceasing. Now is the day of salvation, harden not your heart with the things of this world. Love the heavenly things above. Live in the world but live for God only.

For I am the answer to all things of this world.

Get your eyes on the things above and not on the things of this world. Love the heavenly things above, but let the heavenly things abide in you and God will abide with you. Get your mind on the heavenly things and all these other things will be added unto you.

Ask, and it SHALL be given you; seek, and ye shall find; knock, and it SHALL be opened unto you: For everyone that asketh receiveth; and he that seeketh findeth; and to him that knocketh it SHALL be opened. (Matthew 7: 7 – 8)

But seek ye first the kingdom of God, and his righteousness and all things SHALL be added unto you. For your Father knoweth that ye have need of all these things. Take therefore no thought for the morrow, for the morrow SHALL take thought for the things of itself. Sufficient unto the day is the evil thereof.

Lay not up for yourselves treasures upon the earth, where moth and rust doth corrupt, and where thieves break through and steal. But lay up for yourself treasures in heaven, where neither moth nor rust doth corrupt, and where thieves do not break through nor steal: For where your treasure is there will your heart be also.

DELIVERANCE: GOD'S PROMISE IN THE LAST DAYS

In the last days, my friend, there is deliverance for all those that call upon the name of the Lord. My friend, there is deliverance for all God's people, just believe and claim deliverance in the name of the Lord and deliverance is yours in the name of Jesus. Let the Word of God dwell in your heart and believe with all your heart. Then stand back and watch the salvation of the Lord work in your life.

There SHALL be deliverance for all those that call upon the name of the Lord. For God is the answer to everything, no matter what you need. For nothing is impossible with God to those that believe. Without God we can do nothing. But with God we CAN do anything in the name of the Lord. For God is the Alpha and the Beginning and the Bright and Morning Star.

For what he done in the Bible long ago, he CAN do for you if you will only trust and believe his word. But we must pray without ceasing for time is drawing nigh. For our time on earth will soon be gone. We must pray and fast in order to make it into heaven. But most of all, read the Word of God. For the Bible is a guide to true salvation.

GOD'S MESSAGE TO HIS CHILDREN

In a twinkling of an eye I'll split the Eastern skies. I am coming home to get my children to carry them home. For not even the Angels know of my coming. For only I know the time and the hours. Children, look around for I will show you signs to let you know my time is at hand. Read your Bibles for you will find the signs of my coming. Children watch and pray, for when I come, look toward the Eastern Skies for that is where I am going to send my Angels to bring my children home. Pray you're not asleep when I come or you will not enter into heaven with me.

For I am soon coming. My children don't wait till I've come and gone to get right with me. Now is the time to get right with me. For if I come and you're not right with me you'll get left behind. For everything I've spoke about in your Bibles is true. For I said that I will give you a mansion just for you and I will give that mansion to you when you come into glory with me. I also promised my children a crown of life for those who have done the will of the Father which is in Heaven. A crown you SHALL receive also. Thus saith the Lord thy God.

WORSHIP GOD IN HOLINESS AND BEAUTY

Let's all join together and give praise unto the Lord that is greater than all other Gods here on this earth. For after all, God is our Creator and Maker of all things. He created man from the dust of the ground and took a rib from the man and created a woman. God even created the heavens.

For fear me over all other Gods, for I am greater than all idols of the earth. For worship me in the beauty of holiness, for I reigneth over everything.

For if you have the Lord you shall hate evil. For He preserveth the souls of his saints, he SHALL deliver them out of the hand of wickedness. Rejoice in the Lord ye righteous, give thanks at the remembrance of his holiness.

Life is hard sometimes and we stumble. Sometimes we don't understand the things around us. But then is the time to turn it around. Don't stay in a stumbling state of mind. But look up and don't look down. Put your right foot forward and press on with your life and live each day one day at a time. Remember to make the best of what you have done and trust God and He will bring you through. That is the only way I know to make it in this life. If you want to have a better life, don't forget to put God first with everything and you will have a life more abundant. And you will live a life rich in love. And your life will be easier and simpler each day that you live your life for God.

WATCH AND PREPARE

Let your loins be girded about, and your lights burning; And ye yourselves like unto men that wait for their lord, when he will return from the wedding; that when he cometh and knocketh, they may open unto him immediately.

Blessed are those servants whom the lord when he cometh shall find watching: verily I say unto you, that he shall gird himself, and make them to sit down to meat, and will come forth and serve them. And if he shall come in the second watch, or come in the third watch, and find them so, blessed are those servants.

And this know, that if the Goodman of the house had known what hour the thief would come, he would have watched, and not have suffered his house to be broken through. Be ye therefore ready also: for the Son of man cometh at an hour when ye think not. (Luke 12: 35 – 40)

But and if that servant say in his heart, My lord delayeth his coming; and shall begin to beat the menservants and maidens, and to eat and drink, and to be drunken; the lord of that servant will come in a day when he looketh not for him and at an hour when he is not aware, and will cut him in sunder, and will appoint him his portion with the unbelievers. And that servant, which knew his lord's will, and prepared not himself, neither did according to his will, shall be beaten with many stripes. But he that knew not, and did commit things worthy of stripes shall be beaten with few stripes.

For unto whomsoever much is given, of him SHALL be much required: and to whom men have committed much, of him they will ask the more. I am come to send fire on the earth; and what will I, if it be already kindled? But I have a baptism to be baptized with; and how am I straitened till it be accomplished!

Suppose ye that I am come to give peace on earth? I tell you, Nay; but rather division: For from henceforth there shall be five in one house divided, three against two, and two against three. (Luke 12: 45 – 52)

For yourselves know perfectly that the day of the Lord so cometh as a thief in the night. (I Thessalonians 5:2) But ye, brethren, are not in darkness, that that day should overtake you as a thief. Ye are all the children of light, and the children of the day: we are not of the night, nor of darkness.

Therefore let us not sleep, as do others; but let us watch and be sober. For they that sleep sleep in the night; and they that be drunken are drunken in the night. But let us, who are of the day, be sober, putting on the breastplate of faith and love; and for an helmet, the hope of salvation. (I Thessalonians 5: 4 – 9)

Now we exhort you, brethren, warn them that are unruly, comfort the feebleminded, support the weak, be patient toward all men. See that none render evil for evil unto any man; but ever follow that which is good, both among yourselves, and to all men. Rejoice evermore. (I Thessalonians 5:14 – 16)

Abstain from all appearance of evil. And the very God of peace sanctify you wholly; and I pray God your whole spirit and soul and body be preserved blameless unto the coming of our Lord Jesus Christ. (I Thessalonians 5:22 – 23)

JESUS IS COMING

We're living in the last days, my friend. Look all around you, my friend. The Bible is being fulfilled every day. If you're not ready my friend, I pray that you do get ready. For my friend, read your Bible and you will know some of the things that I am talking about. But pray my friend that you will not have to go through the tribulation. If you're on fire for God and serving him everyday without ceasing, you will not have to go through the tribulation. Tribulation will be a day of great sorrows and suffering, where times will be harder for people to live and serve God. For now, we can worship in the beauty of holiness. But during tribulation days, you will be killed for serving God.

Then there will be the times of the Mark of the Beast. The mark of the beast is coming. To be a Christian in the perilous days will be hard. For you will have to fully trust God for everything. For if you should take this mark in your forehead, you will be marked as a non-Christian. If you should take this mark you will be known as a traitor to God. Pray my friend that you will not be here during tribulation days. But if you serve God every day with all your heart, mind and soul. You will not have to go through these things.

For I am soon coming to receive you unto my bosom of my father. For in the twinkling of an eye I will split the Eastern Skies. Like a thief in the night, I will come in a time when you may not be ready.

Pray my friends that you be ready when He comes. For if you're not ready and looking for him you will be truly left behind. For now is the time to prepare yourselves for His soon coming – which is closer than anyone knows. For be ye ready for that trumpet; for when that trumpet shall blow graves will burst open and they will be called up to be with the Lord. For God will appear in the Clouds on a great white horse to carry you on to be with the Father which is in heaven.

Behold, I stand at the door, and knock: if any man hear my voice, and open the door, I will come in to him, and will sup with him, and he with me. To him that overcometh will I grant to sit with me in my throne, even as I also overcame, and am set down with my Father in his throne. He that hath an ear, let him hear what the Spirit saith unto the churches. (Revelation 3:20 – 22)

Jesus is coming, be ye ready at all times.

My children, I say I will come back. Get ready my children. For I am coming back to receive you unto my bosom. For no one knows the hour or the day. But I am coming back, for I am even at the door. For I am drawing nigh at the door! Thus saith the Lord.

For yea I stand and knock at the door. Waiting for you to call on my name. Do not feel that you are alone. For I am with you always even until the end of the world. For I said I would be with you not just for a day. But I say always, I am the same today, yesterday, and forever. For I am a God that changeth not. What I have done for one, I will do for you. If I can forgive a woman of prostitution I will forgive you also. For I say I am coming. Be ye instant in prayer. For pray ye without ceasing.

Wake up and be ye ready. For that day will come. For I say I am coming. Be ye ready always. For if you're not ready, sanctified and holy, you will be left behind. Watch and pray always. Be ye prepared for my soon coming. For you have heard for years of my coming, but be ye not afraid. For I am soon coming. For I will not let you stay and let you bear more than you can bear. For trust me and you will know. In my spirit I am coming.

For not even the Angels know of my coming, but I am coming to receive you into my bosom. For yea I sit by the Father waiting for God to give me the go ahead. But I wait to wait on God to give me the sign before I can come and receive you. I must wait for everything and every prophecy to be fulfilled. Are you ready should I come this day? Will you be ready for my coming? Pray you're not slumbering and sleeping when I come. For be ye awake and looking for me. Thus saith the Lord!

For this, my friend, is God speaking through me to tell you this, because it is very important that you know what the spirit is saying. So please be ready and willing to go should He come this day. God wants you to prepare yourself for His coming. So search yourself and ask yourself the question, am I really ready to go? If you're not, start getting yourself in order with God. For God is standing with outstretched arms waiting on you to repent, so He CAN come into your heart and dwell forever with you.

Just believe that I died and arose on the third day and repent and I will give you eternal life. Then I can dwell with you for ever and ever.

I do not know the hour or the day my friend, but I pray that you get close to God.

For I am coming. Be ye ready to meet your God. For I would rather have you ready than to see you go through fire and brimstone. For I would rather have you serving me than serving Satan, because I am soon coming. I say again, be ye ready for my soon coming. Be ye clean and white as snow. For there may come a day that it will be too late to make you holy. For I am holy. Be ye holy as I am holy.

Be fired up and filled with the spirit of God. For check yourself and look around you. Make sure, my friend, that you are caught praying and praising God. *For I am coming.* Search yourself and see if your soul is acceptable to God the Father. For God loves you no matter what you have done. Just ask God to forgive you and he will. For there is only one thing that there is no forgiveness of, and that is blaspheming of the Holy Ghost. So don't feel, my friend, that there is no hope for you. Because there is hope for anyone that is athirst after righteousness, he *SHALL* be filled.

For God is the answer and now is the time. Not tomorrow, not next year, but now is the time to get ready for my soon coming. For yea I stand at the door with outstretched arms waiting on you to call on my name.

For my friend, he can be closer than a brother, sister, mother and a father. Just trust God and see if he will not open the windows of heaven to pour you out a blessing that you cannot receive. For God wants to deliver you out of bondage. No matter what it is, God is always there with an open ear, ready to listen to whatever your problem may be.

But call on Jesus in your time of trouble and He will deliver you. For we're in the times where we have got to trust God more than we ever have before. Trust my God with everything and every need in your life will be met.

For I am the Lord thy God that changeth not. I am a God that never changes. I am always the same, yesterday, today and forever. Do not worry about the things that are falling down around you, for I will not allow you to bear more than you can stand to bear. For I would not have you be in the middle of destruction. But I want you to praise me with all your heart, mind and soul. For I am a God that never fails. Be ye clean and white as snow, wearing a robe of righteousness and pure as a glass of water. Thus saith the Lord.

Where any two or three agree together on any one thing, it SHALL be done in Jesus name. I did not say that it wouldn't be done, but I say it SHALL" be done. For nothing is too big or too small that I can't do. Just ask anything in my name and it SHALL be added unto you. For I am a God that does not fail. For all things are possible to those that believe in me. For have faith in me and trust me for all things.

Have faith in me as the grain of a mustard seed. Faith without works is dead, but faith in God prevaileth much. Faith comes by hearing the word of God. The word of God is your strength. When you're in the midst of your troubles, or in the midst of a storm, call on me and I will deliver you. For I will not put on you more than you can bear. I will deliver you out of the midst of the storm. In a time that you thinketh not, I will come in on your behalf and deliver you out of your storm.

The Lord God has power to do all things. Believe that all things are possible through God. For my God is a big God that has power in the palm of His hand to heal the sick, raise the dead, and deliver you out of bondage. For my God is a God of all things. He holds the future in the palm of His hand. He sees all things and He hears everything you do and say.

For pray that your robe is white as snow. For there may come a day that you will have to stand before God at the judgment. Be ye ready for the judgment. For be ye washed up and cleaned up and right with God.

For it will not be man to judge you there. But it will be I the Father of everything. For be ye holy as I am holy. Be ye cleaned up, holy and acceptable unto me. For I am a God that inhabits your praise. Praise in the morning, praise in the noon time, and praise in the evening. I inhabit your praise not just once a week, but every day. Day in and day out praise me always. For I love all of your praise. Praise me in sun, praise me in instruments and praise me in all things. Thank me for everything for I am the one that blesses you with everything you have. For without me you would have nothing.

For I am a God that does not fail. I am the same God yesterday, today, and forever. I am a God that changeth not. But I am a God that owns the cattle of a thousand hills.

Faith comes by hearing the word of God. The word of God fills you with the faith as the grain of a mustard seed. So believe God for a miracle and accept the miracle. For God CAN do all things. For all things are possible to those that believe in the word. For nothing is impossible with God, nothing that He can't do. For my God CAN do all things and anything. Just call on

His name, Jesus, and He will hear you. When you say, Lord, hear my prayer this day, and He will come in on the scene and deliver you out of bondage.

No matter how big, I can move on your behalf. Just call on my name and I will be there for you. For I am a God that holds the future in my hands. Just call on my name and I will deliver you. For anything you ask in my name, you SHALL receive it in Jesus name.

We must always be about our Father's business. Not our earthly father, but our Father which is in heaven. Live day to day going about your Father's business; that is praying and seeking God everyday. If it is preaching, preach the gospel; if it is singing then sing; if it is praying for the sick, then pray for the sick; if it is shouting, then shout; and if it is just saying Amen, then say Amen. Just serve God in the beauty of holiness. Just live day to day staying prayed up and on fire for God. Just live each day the best way you can and work each day serving God.

Glory hallelujah, praise God in the beauty of holiness. Whatever you do for God be sincere and love Him until He comes to get you in the rapture. For He is soon coming to receive you unto His bosom. I do not know the day or the hour, but my Father which is in heaven knows all things. He knows the day and the hour. The Father which is in Heaven knows the day and the hour of His coming. Be ye ready.

EPILOGUE

My daughter was diagnosed with Turners Syndrome and she quit growing at 10 years old. Doctors wanted to give her growth hormones, but God did not allow me to give her growth hormones. Instead I trusted God for a miracle. Debra, my daughter, had decided she did not want the growth hormones herself. Convincing the doctors that I did not believe it was a good idea was difficult, for Debra was a mildly retarded child. God showed me that it would be best to let her grow on her own. She is truly a miracle. She has growed to be 4' 9 1/2 " tall without growth hormones. Doctors said she would only grow to be 4' 7" tall. But the doctors did not know who my God is.

She has growed up to be a beautiful child that graduated from a Trainable Mentally Handicapped (TMH) class with high honors. She graduated and got a job at Food Lion, moved out on her own, and has been living by herself for three years. She has recently married a young man a year older than her who has some of the same problems. They are doing fine. In areas where she is weak, he is strong. But they are living a happy life.

Just because a child is handicapped do not treat that child as a child that can't learn. They can learn if you will work with them. You have to be patient and determined to help.

The love of God is love and gentleness and reaching out to others in times of need. How can you say that you walk in love if you cannot reach out to someone in need? Love is putting yourself to the side for a friend or a loved one. Love is reaching out to the hurting and the burdens of the people.

❧

I told a story about my Dad's problem with alcohol. For years, even after this book was first written, my Dad had a drinking problem. Finally one day it put a toll on his life. Two days after Father's Day, in June of 1998, my Dad got angry with my stepmother and shot her. They had been having marital problems. He had been drinking that day and had gotten angry with her. He had his grandson to bring him his gun. My Dad shot her in the head and she did not survive.

My Dad is in prison for murder. He will have to serve the rest of his life behind bars because of his alcohol and his temper.

So you see, my friend, I know what alcohol does and can do if you don't turn your problems over to God. You may do something that you will live to regret. But going to prison was the best thing that could have happened to him. For he met Jesus and gave his life to God. He realizes now that the alcohol was what had caused him to make mistakes in his life.

The things I had prayed for finally happened. I prayed for my father for years, that he would give his life to God so that we could talk and have peace between us. You see, God knows what He is doing.

Dad, I want you to know I forgive you and I love you. I am very proud of where you are now with God. I have always loved you. Most of all, God loves you too.

If you love God with a Godly love, you will have peace and you will want your love to be reflected through you. Love is being there for a friend or loved one who is in trouble. Love is hope to the hurting and the lost. We must let the light of God shine in our lives so that others can see Jesus in us.

I am the Light and if you love me your light will shine for others to see.

———

My husband has always been a blessing to me. When I was discouraged he would reassure me that God was in control, and that everything was going to be all right. See, my husband has been very supportive of me. Even when I would help family members and bring them in my home, he would support me. Sometimes he would not understand, but he would always give me the benefit of the doubt that I knew what I was doing.

My husband will always be my "knight in shining armor" that rescued me from problems beyond my control. He was my Moses that rescued me from out of bondage. He will always have a special place in my heart. For God has put a special bond between us that not even Satan can destroy. Believe me, he has sure tried. But God has kept us together for 27 years. Through thick and thin we have survived. But I give God the glory for keeping us together all these years.

I hope with all my heart that this book will help you some to understand how to be closer to God. And remember, God loves you!

A WORD ABOUT THE AUTHOR...

Alma is a devoted wife to her husband of 34 years, the mother of two daughters, and a grandmother of two girls. She is an ordained Pentecostal Evangelist minister filled with faith and love for God, anointed by God to preach the gospel. She and her husband plan to start a traveling Miracle Revival Ministry and continue in the path God has given her.

For questions about this book or to order additional books, please contact:

Alma Benefield

472 Azalea Drive

Macclenny, Florida 23063